D0944576

DANCE & FITNESS
TRENDS

YOGA
Fitness

Amie Jane
Leavitt

Mitchell Lane
PUBLISHERS
P.O. Box 196
Hockessin, DE 19707

Mitchell Lane
PUBLISHERS

African Dance Trends
Get Fit with Video Workouts
Line Dances Around the World
Trends in Hip-Hop Dance
Trends in Martial Arts
The World of CrossFit
Yoga Fitness
Zumba Fitness

Printing
1 2 3 4 5 6 7 8 9

Library of Congress
Cataloging-in-Publication Data

Leavitt, Amie Jane.
 Yoga fitness / by Amie Jane Leavitt.
    pages cm. — (Dance and fitness trends)
 Audience: Age 9-13.
 Audience: Grade 4 to 8.
 Includes bibliographical references and index.
 ISBN 978-1-61228-551-1 (library bound)
 1. Hatha yoga—Juvenile literature.
 2. Exercise—Juvenile literature. 3. Mind and body—Juvenile literature. I. Title.
 RA781.7.L435 2015
 613.7'046—dc23
                                    2014006933

eBook ISBN: 9781612285917

Contents

When standing in mountain pose, the body is strong and the mind is quiet. Mountain pose is also called *tadasana*.

Chapter 1
Do I Really Want to Be a Yogi or Yogini?

Lizzie follows her friend Micah up the stairs into the large studio at the community center. It's cozy and warm inside with soft lighting, dark hardwood floors, and a creamy vanilla-colored paint on the walls. The large picture windows on the west side of the room sparkle with golden sunlight. Red, orange, and yellow leaves dance about on the trees outside as the wind softly rustles through them.

It's late afternoon in early autumn and today is the day Lizzie has finally agreed to try her very first yoga class. She's a little worried. Will she like yoga as much as Micah has promised? Will she be any good at it?

"You can put your shoes, socks, and jacket over here," Micah says as he places his own jacket on a hook and kicks his shoes and socks under a long wooden bench. Then as Lizzie puts away her shoes and jacket, Micah opens up one of the cupboards. "Here is a yoga mat for you to use," he says, handing her a long green mat that is rolled up like a tube. "Don't worry," Micah says as he sees the anxious look on her face. "I'll show you how to roll it out and the teacher will show you how to do all the poses. It's going to be fun!"

Micah and Lizzie walk barefoot over to the middle of the room. They unroll their mats and lay them out near each other. "It's best if they're not right next to each other," Micah explains. "That way we will have plenty of room to move our arms and legs out during the poses."

Soon, the rest of the room fills up with mats and people of all ages. Lizzie and Micah are definitely not the youngest, even though she thought they would be. Three second graders,

one third grader, and one fourth grader from their school have set up their mats in the front of the room near the teacher.

"That's Emmaline," Micah says. "She's the teacher."

Emmaline unrolls her mat and places it just below the big picture windows. She slips off her flip-flops and places them by the front wall. Then, she sits down on her mat and speaks to the class. "Do any of you have any concerns you'd like me to know about tonight?" Emmaline has a soft, soothing voice that Lizzie finds very calming and peaceful.

One man in the back raises his hand and says he has a lower back injury. A lady in the front raises her hand and says that she must be careful with her shoulders and neck because of a surgery she had years ago. A young teenager near the door says he recently hurt his knee in football practice.

"Thank you for this information," Emmaline says. "I will make sure I give some extra help to those students as we move through our poses. Oh, I guess I should ask too, is anyone here today for the first time?"

"My friend Lizzie is," Micah announces to the class.

Lizzie shrinks on her mat. She gets a little shy around people she doesn't know. But then instantly Emmaline speaks out to reassure her.

"Welcome, Lizzie," Emmaline says. "Just follow my lead tonight and you will be fine. If you have any questions, be sure to let me know." She gives Lizzie a warm smile. Lizzie smiles back.

Emmaline then walks across the room and puts on some soft music. It reminds Lizzie of the music she hears at the Indian restaurant that her family goes to often. She really likes it. It feels peaceful and relaxing. "*Om, Om, Om,*" the voice chants through the speakers.

"Stand at the top of your mats, students. Your feet should be hip-distance apart. Spread your toes out so they grip the mat. Now, place your arms and hands directly beside your legs. This is mountain pose," Emmaline speaks slowly and clearly in her smooth, calm voice.

Lizzie follows Emmaline's instructions. "This is easy," she thinks to herself. "First pose, done."

"Look down at your fingers and think about the present moment. Forget about all the stress from your day. Let it melt away. Think about what you'd like to accomplish with your yoga practice today. Be mindful of your breath. Let it fill your lungs and warm your body," Emmaline explains. She takes a long deep breath through her nose to demonstrate proper breathing to the class.

This long deep breath reminds Lizzie of the powerful sound of the ocean's waves as they crash on the shore at the beach. She also likes the way it feels when she breathes in so deep that she can almost feel it in her toes!

"Now, as you breathe in, lift your hands up in a big arch towards the sky," Emmaline says. "Look up at your fingertips. Then, as you breathe out, lower them back down as you swan dive into our second pose, the forward bend. Slightly bend your knees and touch your fingertips to the floor if you can. If you can't touch the floor, bend your knees a little more until your fingers are on your mat. We will hold this pose a little longer this time and let you breathe in and out a few breaths."

Lizzie likes the way this pose feels. She felt graceful as she swooped down with her arms in the swan dive. Now, the forward bend is stretching the backs of her legs. She hadn't realized it before, but her legs sure are tense from sitting at her school desk all day long.

"Now, straighten your legs, class," Emmaline instructs. "Then, as you breathe in, straighten your back out like a table. Breath out and return back to forward bend." The class moves into poses called cobra and downward-facing dog. Lizzie can feel both the front and the back of her body stretching in these positions. Emmaline instructs the class to move into a

There are several different ways to do the forward bend, or *uttanasana*. The full pose, like the one shown in the picture, is the most advanced. The knees are kept straight and the hands are completely on the floor. Other modifications can include bending the knees or resting the hands on blocks.

forward bend again. "Now, breathe in and swoop back up for a reverse swan dive. Breathe out and bring your hands back to your side. Congratulations to our first timer, Lizzie. She just completed her very first sun salutation."

Lizzie beams. "My first sun salutation? How cool is this?" she thinks to herself.

Micah can see the happiness on her face. "See, I told you it was fun and easy. You'll like the rest of the practice, too," he smiles back at her.

Micah is right. Lizzie does like the rest of the practice. They do many other kinds of fun poses like tree pose, child's pose, and pigeon. She never knew that yoga had so many fun names for its exercises. It feels like she is playing or creating more than she is working out. Maybe there is something to this yoga after all, she decides.

At the end of the one-hour practice, Lizzie is feeling a little tired from all the poses. Yet her muscles feel energized and long and lean.

Emmaline tells the class to lie down on the floor with their backs flat on their mats. She tells them to just let their arms relax out to their sides with their palms facing up. Their legs should be stretched out flat on the mat. Then, she turns out the lights and closes the blinds of the big picture windows so it's dark in the room.

She speaks in her soothing, calm voice again. "All of you who are familiar with yoga know that this is our favorite part. Those who are new to this practice, let me explain what we're doing now. This is called *shavasana*, or corpse pose. For the next five minutes, I want you to just completely relax. Release all the tension from your toes, your fingertips, your legs, your arms, your back. Relax your face muscles and keep your eyes closed. Relax your breath."

Lizzie feels completely relaxed. In fact, she has never felt so comfortable in her life, not even on her own comfy bed. And here she was lying on a thin rubber mat on a hard wood

In corpse pose, or shavasana, yogis lie on their backs with their arms and legs flat on the mat. This pose, the last one of any yoga practice, is a pose of relaxation.

floor! She feels as though she is floating on a soft, puffy cloud and all the stress from her day has totally disappeared.

She almost drifts off to sleep, but then she hears Emmaline's soft, soothing voice.

"Okay, class, the five minutes is up. It's now time to slowly come out of shavasana. Start to wiggle your fingers and toes. Keep your eyes closed, but slowly roll over to your right side with your legs curled. When you're ready, raise yourself to a seated position with your legs crossed. Now, place your right thumb over your right nostril and breathe through your left nostril. Now, remove your thumb. Take your right index finger over your left nostril and breathe through your right nostril. Slowly open your eyes. I hope you have all met your intentions for your practice today. Go out and have a great rest of the day! I'll see you back here on Thursday. *Namaste*."

The teacher bows to the class from her seated position. Then, she gets up and slowly opens the blinds on the windows.

"So what did you think?" Micah asks Lizzie.

"I loved it!" she replies. "What time is class on Thursday?"

Popularity of Yoga & Fun Yoga Facts

Over the last decade, yoga has become very popular in the United States. In 2008, *Yoga Journal* conducted a study through Sports Marketing Surveys USA. It was found that about 15.8 million people in the United States practiced yoga on a regular basis. Now, fast forward four years to 2012. The same survey was conducted, but by that year, 20.4 million people were practicing yoga on a regular basis and 44.4 percent of the people who were not practicing said they would very much like to get involved in it. Here are some more interesting yoga statistics:

Of the 20.4 million people who were practicing yoga in the United States in 2012,
- 44.8 percent consider themselves beginners (of that number, 22.9 percent are new to yoga while 21.9 percent are beginning to practice yoga again after taking some time off)
- 39.6 percent consider themselves intermediate
- 15.6 percent consider themselves advanced/expert

And, some fun yoga facts.
People are combining yoga with other workouts and hobbies to create new and exciting types of fitness regimes.

Doga: Don't leave Fido at home! Bring him with you to these people- and pet-friendly workouts. Chances are your dog will *love* doing the downward-facing dog!

Yogalates: This workout blends the best of yoga and Pilates together!

Acroyoga: Work together with a friend or classmate to do acrobatic movements as a team.

Acroyoga

Placing the hands at heart's center reminds yogis to be mindful of their practice. That means that they are to think about their breath and their poses and forget about the worries and stresses of their day.

Chapter 2
Thousands of Years Ago and Thousands of Miles Away

Unlike many other fitness programs that have their origins in modern times, yoga actually began many thousands of years ago in a place many thousands of miles away.

The Indus Valley is located in what is today known as Afghanistan, Pakistan, and northwestern India. It extends along the Indus River, which is one of Asia's most important rivers. This area is home to one of humanity's earliest civilizations: the Indus Valley Civilization. At its peak, it's believed that this civilization had a population of over five million. The people of the Indus Valley farmed, built homes out of mud bricks, made handicrafts and artwork out of clay and metal, crafted tools and weapons out of bronze and copper, and traded with other people who lived along the river. And apparently, some of these people also did yoga!

The Indus Valley Civilization existed around five thousand years ago. Archaeologists have discovered stone seals here that they believe were carved by these people. These sculptures are particularly interesting because they are the oldest known pieces of art that show people in yoga poses. This artwork dates back to about 3000 BCE. Beginning in the third century BCE, written texts from northwestern India also described yoga poses, meditation, and the benefits of doing both.

So, exactly what is yoga? Yoga is a philosophy, or way of thinking. The word yoga comes from the Sanskrit language. It means to "yoke" or "unite." This "uniting" has two meanings. First of all, in yoga, it's important for the physical body to become more aware of, or united with, the mind and the

spirit. It's also important for the physical body to become more united with nature, or the universe as a whole.

The most popular path of yoga in the Western world is hatha yoga, which emphasizes physical movements and breath control. Because of that, it's this specific type of yoga that will be focused on throughout the rest of this book.

Hatha yoga includes many different styles, but within all of these styles, the same postures are taught. For example, all hatha styles teach the pose called "downward-facing dog." However, one style might have you move quickly through this pose while another style might have you hold it for a longer length of time and really focus on your alignment (the way your body is positioned) and your breathing.

Here are five examples of different styles of hatha yoga.

Iyengar Yoga

This style of teaching was developed by a man named B.K.S. Iyengar. He is known all over the world as one of the greatest living yogis (people who practice yoga). He spent several decades developing this style.

Iyengar yoga is a therapeutic type of yoga. It is really great for people who have had injuries because it is a slow moving yoga that places emphasis on proper alignment of the muscles and skeleton. In Iyengar yoga, the poses are held for a longer length of time than in most other types of yoga. The idea with this type of yoga is that when the poses are done precisely, the person will develop balance, flexibility, stamina, and improved overall health.

In Iyengar yoga, many different types of props are used, like blankets, straps, blocks, ropes, sandbags, wedges, benches, stools, boxes, and even wooden gymnastic-type horses.

Ashtanga Vinyasa Yoga

This type of yoga is also just called Ashtanga yoga, vinyasa yoga, or flow yoga. It is probably one of the most well-known types of hatha yoga because it's the yoga that is generally offered at fitness gyms. Power yoga is also based on this type of yoga. Ashtanga vinyasa yoga was initially developed by K. Pattabhi Jois in the mid-1900s at his Ashtanga Yoga Research Institute in southern India.

In this type of yoga, students learn a series of postures and perform them in a specific order. The class begins with the sun salutation poses, or as they are called in Sanskrit, *surya namaskara*. In traditional Ashtanga vinyasa yoga, the poses are taught in a primary series, an intermediate series, and four advanced series. Students do not move on to the intermediate series until the poses in the primary series have been mastered. In many gyms, a derivative form is taught that incorporates the same poses, but the teacher has more freedom to arrange the order of the poses. The reason that Ashtanga vinyasa is also called "flow yoga" is because each pose flows smoothly into the next pose until the entire series is finished.

As students complete the poses in Ashtanga vinyasa, they are expected to breathe in a certain way through their noses. It is called the *ujjayi* (ooh-JAI-ee) breath. Ujjayi is a deep breath that fills the entire belly and chest cavity with air and makes an ocean-like sound when it passes over the back of the throat. This breath is supposed to do three things: warm up the body, get oxygen to all areas of the body, and help the person to really focus their awareness on the breath while doing difficult poses.

Ashtanga vinyasa is a very vigorous style of yoga. The students flow through the poses rather smoothly and quickly. Some students claim they get an aerobic workout from doing Ashtanga vinyasa, but health experts generally agree that the practice doesn't escalate the heart rate enough to truly call it a cardio program.

Even the military includes yoga in their exercise regimens. Here, Major Lucy Carillo of the 379th Air Expeditionary Wing Judge Advocate, leads a yoga class in Southeast Asia.

There are many different types of yoga. This particular one, taught at Rain City Yoga in Seattle, is an advanced prana vinyasa class.

Bikram Yoga
Bikram yoga is in one word: intense! The room is kept at a steamy 105°F and 40 percent humidity. Essentially, it feels like you're working out in a sauna! The room is kept this warm for several reasons. For one, it's supposed to mimic the tropical conditions found in southern India, where the Bikram yoga style originated. Second, it's believed that the intense heat helps students achieve greater flexibility in their muscles and joints. This can help prevent injury, and may allow students to achieve longer lasting results. Bikram yoga is particularly great for people who want to increase their flexibility.

There's a whole lot of sweating going on in Bikram yoga, so students have to really be mindful of their bodies to avoid getting ill. Students should bring along plenty of water to drink during their practice and if it gets too hot, they should either stop doing the poses and lie down in child's pose or leave the room for a breath of fresh air.

Bikram yoga was developed by a man named Bikram Choudhury, who brought this style to the United States in the 1970s. It's now practiced in thousands of studios around the world and is particularly popular with movie stars in Hollywood. Classes generally run for ninety minutes and include twenty-six specific poses and two breathing exercises. Teachers also follow a script in Bikram yoga. So, if a person were to attend a class in New York City one day and then another class in Seattle the next, the two classes would be fairly identical.

Viniyoga
Viniyoga was developed by T.K.V. Desikachar in the 1960s, who learned from his father T. Krishnamacharya. It was made popular in the United States by a yoga instructor named Gary Kraftsow in 1999. He founded the American Viniyoga Institute, an organization of people—students and teachers alike—who are dedicated to this type of yoga.

In Viniyoga, classes are small. In fact, sometimes they're just one student per teacher. This is very different from the other yoga teaching styles that often have fifty to one hundred students in one class. Because classes are small, the specific needs of the students (age, physical condition, injuries, and overall health) can be taken into consideration. In Viniyoga, teachers must be constantly thinking about the well-being of their students. For example, throughout a class a teacher might ask himself or herself, "How are the postures helping the students in my class?" If the poses are not helping, then the teacher is expected to adjust the postures accordingly.

Viniyoga is a gentle yoga. An emphasis is placed on seated breathing exercises, chants, mantras, meditation, and spiritual and philosophical teaching.

Kundalini Yoga

Kundalini yoga is the yoga of awareness and is designed for those who truly want a spiritual experience out of their yoga practice. Classes generally include a lot of chanting and singing. Teachers wear white clothing, and often, so do the students. The class usually begins in the seated position. With their eyes closed and hands at heart's center, students go through a series of chants and mantras. Then, the students proceed with a warm up and exercises, and conclude with meditation and relaxation.

Kundalini is often considered an advanced form of yoga and meditation. It was introduced in the United States by Yogi Bhajan in 1969.

Six Paths of Yoga

There are many different yoga paths. Some are focused more on meditation. Some are focused more on scriptural learning and prayer. Some are focused on physical poses. And some are focused on wisdom and the intellect. Here are six of the most well-known yoga paths:

Jnana Yoga—yoga path that is dedicated to achieving wisdom and knowledge through contemplation, meditation, and the questioning of preconceived beliefs.

Bhakti Yoga—yoga path that is dedicated to creating a connection to God through devotion, love, compassion, and prayer.

Karma Yoga—yoga path that is dedicated to creating a connection to God through service to others and selfless actions.

Mantra Yoga—yoga path that is devoted to sacred verses or mantras that are repeated aloud as a form of meditation.

Raja Yoga—yoga path that focuses on self-control of the mind and body through poses, breath control, and meditation.

Hatha Yoga—yoga path that includes physical control and includes a series of physical postures, breathing exercises, cleansing processes, and mindful awareness.

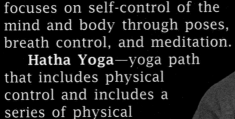

Tree pose, or *vrksasana*, is a balancing pose. While standing in this pose, a person should find something stationary (like a spot on a wall, or a branch on a tree) to focus on.

Chapter 3
How Are a Pigeon, a Cobra, and a Downward-Facing Dog Alike?

So far in this book, there has been a lot of talk about "poses." What exactly is a pose? In yoga, a pose is a way of positioning the body. Poses are also called "postures." In Sanskrit, yoga poses are called *asanas*. There are many poses in yoga that a person learns and masters over years of practice.

With that explanation of poses, let's move on to answer the question "posed" in the title of this chapter:

How are a pigeon, a cobra, and a downward-facing dog alike?

The answer is: They're all yoga poses! And in fact, they're some of the most common yoga poses that yogis and yoginis learn early on in their yoga practice.

The most important part of doing poses in yoga is remembering to really focus on proper alignment and breathing. You also don't want to force anything. If you feel pain, stop.

Here are descriptions of some basic yoga poses:

Tree
This is a balancing pose. It helps calm your mind while it strengthens the muscles in your legs and feet.

HERE'S HOW TO DO IT: Stand on the ground with your feet hip-width apart. Your legs are straight and your arms are straight down hanging beside your legs. Your weight should be equally balanced between your two feet. Then, shift your balance to the right foot. Lift the left knee in front of you and hold onto it with your hands. Remove your hands. Rotate the knee outwards to the left as far as you can without turning your hips.

Place the sole of your left foot on your right inner thigh (or inner calf if you can't reach your thigh yet). Find a spot on the wall to focus on so you don't lose your balance. In Sanskrit, this is called your *drishti*, or focus point. Place your hands together at heart's center, in a "praying" position in front of your heart. Don't take your eyes off your drishti. Hold the pose while breathing in and out several times. Don't worry if you fall, just try again! Then, slowly lower your leg and repeat with the other side.

Cobra

This pose helps stretch your back, neck, chest, and shoulders. It's supposed to look like a cobra getting ready to strike.

HERE'S HOW TO DO IT: Lie face down. Legs should be straight out. Bend your arms so your elbows are next to your ribs. Place your hands on the ground with your fingers near your shoulders. Breathe in and gently start to push your upper body off the ground while slowly straightening your arms (you may not be able to straighten your arms completely; don't force it). Keep your neck long. Pull your shoulders down and back. Feel the stretch in your back, your neck, your chest, and your shoulders.

Child's Pose

This is a good pose to go into during a yoga practice if the other poses get too difficult and you just need to take a break. It's a relaxing pose yet also helps develop flexibility in the ankles, feet, and hips.

HERE'S HOW TO DO IT: Kneel on the floor. Ankles should be close together, and knees should be as wide as your hips. Sit back on your heels. Fold over and place your forehead on the ground. Tuck your arms next to your legs, or stretch your arms out in front of you if you'd like to stretch your lower back.

Pigeon

This pose is a great one to open up the hips and stretch the lower pelvic muscles.

HERE'S HOW TO DO IT: Kneel on all fours. Place your hands directly under your shoulders and your knees below your hips. Bring your right knee forward until it touches your right wrist. Rotate your shin and foot inwards towards your left arm. Straighten out the back leg. Lower down until you're resting on the hip of the right leg and the upper quad of your left leg. Be careful not to lean to one side; your hips should be level. Now, walk your hands forward and lower your upper body to rest on your forearms. If you feel comfortable there, you can stretch further by resting your forehead on the mat. You should feel the stretch in the top of your left

thigh and the outside of your right hip. Repeat with your other leg.

Downward-Facing Dog

This pose looks just like its namesake! It is a fantastic one to help stretch your hips, hamstrings, shoulders, arms, back, and essentially the majority of your body. It is a common pose in yoga and one you'll do many times during a typical practice.

HERE'S HOW TO DO IT: Start on all fours with your knees directly below your hips and your toes curled under. Your hands should be slightly in front of your shoulders. Spread your fingers out wide, so your hands can touch more of the floor or mat. Slowly lift your knees away from the floor and push your hips high towards the

ceiling. Your feet should be hip-width apart from each other. Your knees should still be slightly bent and your heels off the ground. Pull your shoulder blades back and keep your arms straight. Your body should be forming an upside down "V." Take several breaths in this pose. Try to straighten your legs and lower your heels to the floor or mat if you can. If you can't, no problem. You will become more flexible over time.

Bridge Pose
This pose is a fantastic one to build strength in your lower back, legs, and abdominals. It is a precursor to the wheel pose (full backbend).

HERE'S HOW TO DO IT: Lie on your back with your knees bent. Heels should be as close to your sit bones as possible. Arms should be at your sides. Feet should be hip-width apart and parallel to each other. As you exhale, press your feet into the floor and lift your hips off the floor. You should now be resting almost completely on your shoulders and feet. Imagine your body is making a bridge. Pull in your lower back and abdominals (belly

Bridge pose

muscles). Now, place your hands on the floor directly underneath your hips. Clasp your hands together and stretch your arms out long. Stay in this pose for thirty seconds to a minute if you can. Then, slowly move your arms back to your sides and lower your hips to the floor. Move your knees together and rest. Try to do it several times in a row if you can. Be careful not to strain your neck; always keep the neck relaxed.

Corpse Pose

This is also called relaxation pose or, in Sanskrit, shavasana (see page 10 in Chapter 1). This pose is always the last pose of any yoga practice and is one that people look forward to throughout their entire practice. With this pose, the body gets to truly relax. It's best to have the lights off for this one, or place a towel or piece of clothing over your eyes.

HERE'S HOW TO DO IT: Lie on your back with your feet apart, slightly wider than your hips. Your legs can be flat on the ground, or if you prefer, you can bend your knees and place a blanket or block under them. Your arms are resting on the floor, stretched out to your sides with your palms facing skyward. Close your eyes. Relax your feet. Relax your ankles. Relax your hands, your fingers, your arms, and your legs. Relax your face, your neck, your shoulders, and your back. Relax every part of your body. Allow your breath to be soft and slow. Stay in this pose for five to ten minutes. To come out of shavasana, slowly start to wiggle your fingers and toes. Allow the sensation to come back into all areas of your body. When you're ready, roll over to your right side with your knees bent. Then, slowly push yourself up into a seated position with your legs crossed, keeping your eyes closed the entire time.

How Can I Get Started?

The best way to learn how to do yoga is in a class. Yoga classes are taught in many different types of places such as yoga studios, fitness gyms, community centers, art centers, dance studios, and even some public schools. If you aren't able to go to a class, no worries. You can also learn how to do yoga on television or the Internet. There are many great DVDs out there that demonstrate yoga. You can buy these at a store or online, or you can check them out from your local library. You can also watch YouTube videos or entire yoga classes online. Try the *Total Body Workout* series with Deni Preston or the Do Yoga With Me website that features videos with a variety of teachers. Take a look at the "On the Internet" section in the back of this book for the links to those sites. You can check out books from the library that teach you how to do yoga, too.

You do not need any special kind of equipment to do yoga. You just need to wear comfortable clothing that is easy to move in. Since you will be in a variety of positions, it's good to wear clothing that is form-fitting enough to stay in place, but not so tight that it will make moving difficult. If you prefer loose-fitting clothing like a t-shirt, you may wish to also wear a tank top underneath. Sleeveless tops are good, since you will be moving your arms in many directions. Yoga pants or shorts are good options for bottoms, and many people like to arrive in shoes that are easy to slide on and off, like flip-flops. It's also best to have a yoga mat (although many gyms and studios will provide one for you). These help you do the poses more easily because they prevent you from sliding around on the ground when your hands and feet get sweaty. Mats can be purchased at a variety of places (including fitness and department stores) for as little as $10-$12. But if you don't have a mat, don't let that stop you. Yoga can be done with or without a mat!

People who practice yoga do so for many reasons. While yoga strengthens the body and can improve overall health, it can also reduce stress.

Chapter 4
Yoga: The Strengthening of Body, Mind, and Spirit

Yoga philosophy teaches that a person is made up of three parts. First, there is the physical body. Second, there is the mind or brain. Third, there is the soul. Throughout the practice of yoga, all three parts of the person are developed or strengthened. After all, yoga means to "yoke" or "unite." So, the regular practice of yoga helps to unite all three parts of the person.

This is a fairly unique concept for an exercise program. Most programs just focus on developing or strengthening the physical part of a person. Granted, all forms of exercise do improve a person's overall well-being as a natural consequence of improving one's health. However, yoga is unique because it clearly states that intention—of uniting mind, body, and spirit—up-front as its main goal.

Because of this focus, there are many health benefits associated with doing yoga. People often feel more calm and less stressed after attending just one class. They feel less worried about future events in their lives because they have come to realize the importance of focusing on the present moment (a key principle of yoga). They also have an improved ability to concentrate and focus on their tasks outside of yoga. Many people also notice that their physical ailments start to improve, too. For example, people who get severe headaches often find that they experience fewer headaches after practicing yoga regularly. Because a person's flexibility increases, he or she experiences fewer injuries when doing other activities. Research also shows that yoga can help to lower a person's blood pressure. It can improve strength and balance. It can help people deal with depression and emotional issues, too.

People decide to try yoga for many reasons. A study conducted by *Yoga Journal* in 2012 found the top five reasons that people began practicing yoga: 78.3 percent wanted more flexibility; 62.2 percent wanted to achieve general conditioning; 59.6 percent wanted stress relief; 58.5 percent wanted improved overall health; and 55.1 percent wanted to achieve physical fitness.

Josh Ogzewalla, who is now a certified yoga instructor, started practicing yoga "as a way to manage some very specific health issues," he explained. "Western medicine only goes so far, and I wanted a more holistic approach."

Deni Preston, a fitness instructor for more than twenty-five years, also decided to try yoga for similar reasons. "I developed an autoimmune illness named transverse myelitis that attacked my spinal cord and had me in a wheelchair overnight. Because of this, I turned to yoga for rehabilitation and during the process found my passion for it. It reinspired me to help myself and others. It empowered me to live in my body with sensitivity. It also relieved my chronic physical and emotional pain—I no longer need that wheelchair! It helped me to overcome and heal my body, my mind, and my spirit. It became play for me in a very stressful world of raising children, working, and the day-to-day stresses of life."

Another great benefit of yoga is that people of all ages can get involved. Connie Day, a yoga instructor in New York City, has been teaching yoga since 2006. For more than three of those years, she taught classes specifically for children. "I taught in all kinds of settings: studios, art centers, community centers, and even public schools. The children in my youth classes were as young as three and as old as twelve or thirteen. Once they reached the older pre-teen years, I enrolled them in my teen or adult classes because they oftentimes felt more comfortable there," she stated. As she taught the children in

Connie Day is a yoga instructor in New York City. She believes that kids can also enjoy the benefits of a yoga practice, even if they don't enjoy most competitive sports. Here, she demonstrates triangle pose, or *trikonasana*, which builds strength, balance, and stability.

her classes, she was able to help them relax and focus on the present moment. She also helped them understand that exercise can be fun. Most poses have the names of animals,

anyway, but when she had the children do the poses, she really let them "act" out the parts. "When they did cobra pose, I had them *hiss* like a snake. And when they did downward-facing dog, they could let out a few *barks!*"

During her time as a yoga teacher for kids, Connie was very excited to see that many children—who don't necessarily enjoy traditional sports—really thrive in yoga. "That's the great thing about yoga," she explained. "There's no competition. People in yoga are supposed to focus on their own practice and not worry about being better at a pose than their neighbor. Most sports are focused solely on competition. Yoga, instead, is focused on the individual and his or her personal development. This really helps all children improve in their yoga practice because they are in a safe and secure environment."

People find that when they do yoga, many other parts of their lives are affected positively. Adults find that they are able to be more calm in stressful situations. They can be more productive at their jobs and can focus on difficult tasks. Kids also benefit by including a regular yoga practice into their lives.

Atlanta teacher Chelsea Jackson conducted a study with her third grade class. She noticed the students had trouble paying attention in class, and they argued frequently. She had just started doing yoga herself and thought that maybe some of what she was learning could help her students, too. So, she taught them some breathing exercises and a few simple yoga poses. During each school day, the class would take a break from sitting at their desks and get up and practice yoga for a short time. By the end of the year, she noticed many improvements in her class. The students had fewer arguments with each other. They seemed to be better at making decisions throughout the day. They could concentrate better and remember more of the things they learned. They were able to make better use of their class time. They also had increased self-esteem.

Susan Solvang, executive director of K-12 Yoga in Milwaukee, also saw similar benefits with students in her yoga program. Teachers noticed that their students began acting more respectfully at school. The students themselves were even more aware of how loudly they were speaking and if the tone of their voices sounded harsh or mean. When they felt they were speaking that way, they would change it. By the end of the year, they had definitely improved their behavior at school. The school staff kept track of all the "disruptions" or "problems" in the school before the yoga program was implemented, and during its first year. This is what they found:

Benefits of Yoga in Schools	
Year Before Yoga Was Started: 2009-2010	Year Yoga Was Started: 2010-2011
classroom disruptions: 225	classroom disruptions: 110
disorderly conducts: 320	disorderly conducts: 40
fights: 150	fights: 52

After reading about all the benefits of yoga, it's easy to see why so many people have included it in their daily lives. The great thing about yoga is that you don't need to attend a class to do it. You can even benefit by doing the poses here and there throughout your day. Say you have a big test that you have to take at school. Before the teacher passes out the exams, close your eyes at your desk and do some deep breathing exercises. Be mindful of your breath—or in other words—really think about your breath and only your breath. Don't think about the test and your fears about it. Just think about your breathing and how the oxygen is filling every part of your body. Relax your fingers, your toes, your face muscles. After a few deep breaths like this, open up your eyes. Focus your intention on doing the very best you can on your test, and then move forward and do it.

Once you've learned some of the basics of yoga in a class, you can use what you've learned outside of class in a variety of situations.

You can even do yoga poses when you first get up in the morning or before you go to bed at night. Instructor Deni Preston encourages her students to put yoga to use in all kinds of situations. One of her students did just that when she had to take a red-eye (overnight) flight. Airplane seats aren't known to be extremely comfortable, especially on overnight flights. But this student was determined to have a positive experience. She put on an eye mask to cover her eyes, sat in a relaxed position that she called a "seated shavasana." Then, she focused on completely relaxing and "melting" into her seat. She focused on her breath and on relaxing her neck, legs, and arms. She imagined she was lying in her comfortable bed at home and before she knew it, she was asleep. She had a restful night even though she was sitting in that uncomfortable airplane seat. She found out that you can experience the benefits of yoga anytime, anyplace, anywhere.

How Do People Benefit from Doing Yoga?

Here's what two yoga instructors had to say:

Josh Ogzewalla: Yoga helps maintain flexibility and muscle tone. It also helps a person get centered in the "now." In this modern age, we have any number of distractions that keep us from really focusing on the things that are most important. The sense of mindfulness that is attained in yoga allows us to sidestep common missteps in a time of addictions, quick fixes, and instant gratification.

Deni Preston: Yoga helps to facilitate an inner unfolding in each student since it is the fusion of mind, body, and spirit. The students are led to a sweet place where their hearts can open naturally, where they will feel empowered, and are filled with the self-love that so many of us lack. That is the basis of yoga. The asanas, or postures, are vehicles that get us there. The performance of the postures really reflects mindfulness, attitude, balance, strength, flexibility, knowledge, and more. Attitude is always more important than other categories of performance, such as strength and flexibility. Feeling good in one's own skin and accepting "what is" is a wonderful lesson to learn; then progression can begin.

Yoga is something that families can practice at home together, just like this mother and son are doing outside on their deck.

Chapter 5
Taking Your Practice to the Next Level

Let's fast forward in time. You have taken the "plunge" into yoga and have been practicing it for some time now. You love how it makes you feel and you're excited to get even more serious about your practice. You want to know: *What are some ways that I can take my yoga practice to the next level?*

Tara Fraser, yoga instructor and author of the book *Total Yoga*, recommends three ways to deepen your yoga practice. First, she suggests that you start reading books about yoga. Congratulations! Since you chose this book from the shelf and have made it all the way to chapter five, you have already accomplished that first step! Don't stop here, though. Look for other books on yoga. Read magazine articles about it. Learn more about the history of yoga. Learn about what the "big names" in yoga are doing today in their practices. Find out as much as you can about the topic. Second, Fraser suggests that you try to take new types of classes on occasion. You could try out different styles like Bikram yoga or kundalini yoga. If you can't get to a class, then check out some DVDs at the library or participate in some online classes. Third, and most importantly, practice yoga! You can't get better at something if you don't practice. If a piano player wants to play a piece of classical music, he or she certainly can't accomplish that by just sitting the music on the piano and then walking away. The same is true about yoga. If you want to get better at the poses, then you must do them regularly. If you want to get better at breathing techniques and calming your mind, then you must do that often—every day if you can.

Another way to further your practice is by becoming a teacher yourself! Many yoga instructors say that the best thing they did for their own practice was becoming a certified teacher. After practicing yoga for a period of time, that's what Josh Ogzewalla found. "I wanted to take my practice to a deeper level," he explained. "Plus, I also wanted to help others with similar interests and health concerns reap the benefits of yoga in their lives."

So how does one become an instructor? There are many programs throughout the country that provide this training. Some courses require two hundred hours of class time and others require five hundred hours of class time. At successful completion, students have a certificate or diploma that says they are a "200-hour" or "500-hour" instructor. In these classes, students learn all about the history and philosophy of yoga, basic human anatomy, the various teaching styles of yoga, and how to help avoid injuries while doing yoga. Of course, most importantly, students in teacher-training courses also get experience teaching classes, too.

After students finish their teacher training, they are ready to enter the workforce. But what kinds of places hire yoga instructors? Well, the options are many, especially since yoga has become so popular in recent years. Certified teachers can get jobs in fitness gyms, in small yoga studios, at community centers, art centers, dance studios, or public schools. They can also start their own studio, or even just offer classes to family and friends.

Deni Preston has been a fitness instructor in Provo, Utah, for more than twenty-five years. During that time, she has taught many different types of fitness routines, and yoga was just one of those. She taught these classes at local universities and even made fitness videos that were broadcast both on television and on the Internet. Yoga instructor Emily Harper also teaches classes at local universities. Josh Ogzewalla taught family and friends privately. And Connie Day has taught yoga at many different locations including small and large yoga studios, community centers, art centers, public schools, and even at private homes for family and friends.

The pay for yoga instructors varies by location. Some yoga instructors can make $30 or $40 for a half-hour class and much more for longer ones. Others who have their own studio make a set amount per student. This can earn them a lot of money if a large number of students come to their classes. However, this money isn't all profit! Other things have to be taken into consideration, too, like the cost to own or rent the studio, the cost of electricity and other utilities, and the cost of yoga mats and supplies for the studio. If you decide to become a yoga instructor or open your own yoga studio, you'll want to take some classes or read books on business management, too. After all, you will be running your own small business.

Another way that people can make a career out of teaching yoga is by uploading their own videos to YouTube. Anyone can make a YouTube video with very little cost involved. The only problem is that there are many videos out there and yours can get lost in the sea of media if it doesn't stand out from the rest. However, if yours is really good and you get lots of hits, then companies might start paying you to advertise on your video. People can make a good living doing this. Of course, the key to being successful at this is that your video has to be good! Well, it doesn't just have to be *good*, it really has to be *fantastic!* If it's not, no one will watch your video and no companies will advertise, which in the end means no money for you! Being successful at YouTube requires hard work, creativity, and research. If this is an avenue you're interested in, then read articles and books on creating YouTube videos to see what the experts recommend.

Besides becoming an instructor, there are other ways to take your yoga practice to the next level. One way is to learn more about the benefits of a yoga diet. According to yoga philosophy, proper eating includes a diet that is filled with foods in their natural or raw state. So, eating an apple is much better than eating an apple pie! It's also best to eat foods that aren't heavily processed. Eating whole grain wheat bread is better than eating a slice of white bread. Also, some people who practice yoga are vegetarians, which means they don't eat meat. However, not all are. So, don't feel like you can't be a yogi or yogini just because you like to eat meat. But remember that many people who practice yoga do try to be mindful of what they eat, and incorporate as many plant-based foods into their meals as they can. Another key component of a healthy yoga diet is plenty of water. Our bodies are made up of about 50 to 70 percent water. So, it's important that we drink enough water every day to keep our organs—like our brains, hearts, lungs, and kidneys—functioning properly. The amount of water you need daily depends on your age, size, how active you are, your current health conditions, and where you live. Generally speaking, you should drink at least eight (eight-ounce) glasses of water every day. Keep in mind, though, that some people need more and some people need less. Get to know your body and do what's best for YOU.

Overall, adding yoga to your life can help you in many ways. It can give you a fun new outlet to "play" while you add movement to your day. It can help you feel more calm in your daily life. It can give you tools to deal with stressful situations. It can help your physical body become stronger and more flexible. It can help you improve your diet because you've become more "mindful" of the things you eat.

Are you interested in trying yoga? Then, be like Lizzie and just give it a try! Or, if you're already a yogi or yogini, be like Micah, and take your friends to a class to introduce them to the joys of this ancient practice.

Let's spread the love of mind, body, and spirit by doing yoga one day at a time!

Who Is Yoga For?

Emily Harper: Yoga is for everyone, from new baby walkers to the older generations (who may need to use walkers)! Children can benefit from yoga in some of the same ways that adults do. They can improve physical coordination, strength, balance, and flexibility which will greatly enhance their abilities in sports and other activities. It can teach them how to understand their bodies and their feelings in a way that will help them to articulate their needs better (I'm hungry, I'm tired, I've had too much junk and I don't feel well, I need a break, etc.) It can help calm anxieties or hyperactivity. And it can just be plain fun! If it's fun, it brings kids joy. And kids should be happy! It can also teach them how to have patience with themselves and learn not to compare their abilities or limitations with other kids.

Yoga is individual and specific, and with regular practice it really helps us to let go of our egos and have greater concern for being our best selves! Yoga brings balance to my life. It also brings perspective. Not only does it feel good to complete a yoga practice, but real whole-soul healing takes place with consistent yoga practice. My body starts telling me when it has been too many days since my last practice. That intuition is something that is definitely refined with regular practice. It is empowering to practice yoga and to feel more connected to one's self as well as to feel more connected to mother earth, other people, and most importantly to the Divine.

Getting started in anything is half the battle. However, before you embark on any quest in yoga (or anything else for that matter), sit down and talk it over with your parent or guardian. Get their A-Okay before you start hunting down yoga classes on your own! Once you have taken care of this preliminary step, you're free to move on to the following four stops:

First Stop: Your Own Community

If you're interested in practicing yoga, start looking around your own community first. Answer these questions:

1. Are there yoga studios in your community?
2. Are there dance studios in your community?
3. Are there community centers?
4. Are there fitness gyms?
5. Are there art centers?

Any of these places could offer yoga classes. Check out their websites, call them on the phone, or visit them in person. Find out whether they have yoga classes just for kids, or whether kids are allowed to attend beginners' classes. Find out about the pricing (is it per class or per month?). Also, find out whether you will need your own mat, or if one will be provided.

Second Stop: Your School

If there aren't any opportunities to take yoga classes in your community, why not talk to your teacher or principal? Maybe if they knew that kids were interested in such a program, they would look into offering it during the regular school day or even as an after-school program.

Third Stop: Your Library

If you run into a dead-end in stops one and two, then go to your school or public library. Look for books on yoga that you can check out. Search for DVDs or videos that you can borrow. Talk to the librarian. Maybe he or she knows of someplace in your community that offers yoga classes. The librarian might even think it's such a great idea that he or she might decide to use one of the study rooms in the library to hold yoga classes once or twice a week. You never know. The answer is always "no" if you don't ask!

Fourth Stop: The Internet

If Stops One, Two, and Three are fruitless, then hop online. You'll definitely find some yoga resources here. Do a Google search for "Yoga Videos for Kids," or "Online Yoga Class for Kids." You can also search YouTube, or check the websites listed in "On the Internet" on page 45.

Further Reading

Books

Buckley, Annie. *The Kids' Yoga Deck: 50 Poses and Games*. San Francisco, CA: Chronicle Books, 2006.

Chryssicas, Mary Kaye. *Breathe: Yoga for Teens*. New York: DK Publishing, 2007.

Flynn, Lisa. *Yoga for Children: 200+ Yoga Poses, Breathing Exercises, and Meditations for Healthier, Happier, More Resilient Children*. Avon, MA: Adams Media, 2013.

Freeman, Donna. *Once Upon a Pose: A Guide to Yoga Adventure Stories for Children*. Victoria, BC: Trafford Publishing, 2009.

Harper, Jennifer Cohen. *Little Flower Yoga for Kids*. Oakland, CA: New Harbinger Publications, 2013.

Recommended DVDs

Kids World Yoga. Bridget Van Block, 2012.

Shanti Generation: Yoga Skills for Youth Peacemakers. WSR Creative, 2009.

Teen Yoga. Hannover House, 2008.

Yoga for Families. Bayview Entertainment, 2009.

On the Internet

TO FIND INFORMATION ON YOGA:

Gaiam Life: Yoga Answers and Solutions Go-To Guide
http://life.gaiam.com/guides/yoga-answers-and-solutions-go-guide

Green Yoga Association
http://www.greenyoga.org/

MindBodyGreen
http://www.mindbodygreen.com/

Teens Health from Nemours: Yoga
http://kidshealth.org/teen/food_fitness/exercise/yoga.html

Whole Living
http://www.wholeliving.com/

Yoga Journal
http://www.yogajournal.com/

Yoganonymous
http://yoganonymous.com/

Yoga: The Art of Meditation, Breathing, Relaxation, and Spirituality
http://iml.jou.ufl.edu/projects/fall05/levy/history.html

YoKid: What is Yoga for Kids?
http://yokid.org/for-kids/

RECOMMENDED ONLINE CLASSES:

BYU TV: *Total Body Workout*
http://www.byutv.org/show/10507189-2016-4222-baa6-ce44cb446bdf/total-body-workout

Cosmic Kids: Yoga, Stories, and Fun
http://www.cosmickids.co.uk/

Do Yoga With Me
http://www.doyogawithme.com/

Works Consulted

Bergen, Jenna. "Hot Yoga Changed My Life." *Prevention*, February 2013. pp. 56–63.

Carofano, Jennifer. "A-List Advocate." *Natural Health,* June 2012. pp. 32–36.

Collins, Amy Fine. "Planet Yoga." *Vanity Fair*, June 2007. pp. 192-211.

Day, Connie. Personal interview with author, October 2013.

Fraser, Tara. *Total Yoga*. London: Duncan Baird Publishers, 2001.

Harper, Emily. Personal interview with author, October 2013.

Isaacs, Nora. "Yoga Basics." *Natural Health,* November/December 2012. pp. 82–85.

Liao, Sharon. "Yoga." *Real Simple,* May 2013. p. 135.

Mackenzie, Natalie Gingerich. "The Right Yoga Style For You." *Prevention,* October 2011. pp. 32–35.

Martin, Claire. "Flex Benefits." *Los Angeles Magazine*, October 2013. pp. 132–134.

O'Connor, Siobhan. "Christy Turlington Burns: A Yogi, Mother, and Model on a Mission." *Prevention,* September 2013. pp. 96–99.

Ogzewalla, Josh. Personal interview with author, October 2013.

Power, Teresa Anne. "Could Yoga Be the Answer?" *USA Today Magazine,* September 2013. pp. 29–31.

Preston, Deni. Personal interview with author, October 2013.

Schrenk, Sarah Rentz. "Keeping a Healthy Heart with Yoga." *American Fitness*, November/December 2012. pp. 30–31.

Steinmetz, Katy. "Yoga Fusion." *Time*, July 1, 2013. p. 17.

Wertheimer, Kate. "Your Best Yoga." *Natural Health*, September/October 2012. pp. 85–87.

Williamson, Lisa Ann. "Yoga in Public Schools." *Education Digest*, January 2013. pp. 35–37.

Yoga Journal. "New Study Finds More than 20 Million Yogis in US." Yoga Buzz, December 5, 2012.

aerobic (ai-ROH-bik)—Related to exercises that increase the heart rate for an extended period of time, strengthening the heart and lungs and allowing the body to make better use of the oxygen it receives.

asana (AH-suh-nuh)—A pose or position in yoga.

cardio (KAR-dee-oh)—Aerobic exercise.

drishti (DRIH-shtee)—A focal point for the gaze to rest in yoga in order to maintain balance and focus. A drishti could be a spot on a wall, the end of your nose, or your fingertips.

mantra (MAHN-truh)—Specific sound or word(s) used in yoga, like the sound "Om." Its purpose is to focus and transform the mind.

namaste (nah-mah-STAY)—A bowing gesture that is done with hands in prayer at the heart's center as a form of respect and gratitude. In Sanskrit, literally "I bow to you."

Om (AWM)—A singular sound that is meant to focus the mind and prepare it for meditation. It is said to be the original mantra from which all the other mantras were formed.

prana (PRAH-nuh)—Life energy.

pranayama (PRAH-nuh-YAH-muh)—Breathing awareness and control taught in yoga.

shavasana (shah-VAH-sah-nah)—The corpse pose; final pose of a yoga workout in which the person relaxes and receives the benefits of their practice.

sit bones—The bones that protrude from the bottom of the pelvis and are used for sitting.

vinyasa (vin-YAH-suh)—Yoga poses linked to breathing that are performed one after another in a flow of movement.

ujjayi (ooh-JAI-ee)—Loud breathing in yoga that sounds similar to the ocean and is meant to calm and warm the body.

yogi (YOH-gee)—Someone who practices yoga. The term traditionally refers to someone who is devoted to the path of yoga in all aspects of his or her life.

yogini (YOH-guh-nee)—A female yogi.

PHOTO CREDITS: All design elements from Thinkstock/Sharon Beck; Cover, p. 1—Photos.com/Thinkstock; pp. 4, 8, 11, 12, 21, 22, 24, 25, 26, 27, 30, 37, 38, 43—Thinkstock; p. 10—Frances M. Roberts/Newscom; pp. 16-17—Staff Sgt. Joel Mease; p. 18—Benjamin Benschneider/MCT/Newscom; p. 33—Connie Day; p. 36—Airman 1st Class Lauren-Taylor Levin.

Index

About the Author

Amie Jane Leavitt is an accomplished author, researcher, and photographer. She graduated from Brigham Young University as an education major and has since taught all subjects and grade levels in both private and public schools. She is an adventurer who loves to travel the globe in search of interesting story ideas and beautiful places to capture in photos. She has written more than fifty books for kids, has contributed to online and print media, and has worked as a consultant, writer, and editor for numerous educational publishing and assessment companies. Amie has been practicing yoga since 2006. Since the first time she tried it, she knew she loved it so much that she was going to continue practicing it for the rest of her life. Because of that, she particularly enjoyed researching and writing this book and hopes that those who read it will gain a greater appreciation for yoga and a desire to practice it as well. To check out a listing of Amie's current projects and published works, check out her website at www.amiejaneleavitt.com.